STRIDERS

Ice Rescue

⚊SCHOLASTIC

Published in the UK by
Scholastic Education, 2024
Scholastic Distribution Centre, Bosworth Avenue,
Tournament Fields, Warwick, CV34 6UQ
Scholastic Ireland, 89E Lagan Road, Dublin Industrial
Estate, Glasnevin, Dublin, D11 HP5F

1 2 3 4 5 6 7 8 9   4 5 6 7 8 9 0 1 2 3

Printed by Ashford Colour Press

This book is made of materials from
well-managed, FSC®-certified forests
and other controlled sources.

MIX
Paper from
responsible sources
FSC
www.fsc.org   **FSC® C011748**

A CIP catalogue record for this book is available from
the British Library.

ISBN 978-0702-32730-8

Author
Zoë Clarke

Editorial team
Rachel Morgan, Vicki Yates, Alison Gilbert,
Jennie Clifford

Design team
Dipa Mistry, Andrea Lewis and We Are Grace

Photographs
p4 (background) vectorpouch/Shutterstock

Illustrations
Ana Latese/The Bright Agency

How to use this book

This book practises these letters and letter sounds:

y (as in 'funny')	ea (as in 'sweater')	wh (as in 'whale')
ow (as in 'window')	g (as in 'giant')	le (as in 'cable')
al (as in 'metal')	c (as in 'ice')	o-e (as in 'some')
ce (as in 'fence')		

Here are some of the words in the book that use the sounds above:

chilly   headed   danger   white   entrance

This book uses these common tricky words:

the of were there's said to our they was one who called working your are through water pull

About the series

This is the third of three books featuring a team of underwater explorers who have adventures on their mini-submarine. Their mission is to clean up the oceans and to protect them.

Before reading

- Read the title and look at the cover. Discuss what this book might be about?
- Talk about the characters on page 4 and read their names.
- The story is split into chapters shown by numbers at the top of the page.

During reading

- If necessary, sound out and then blend the sounds to read the word: g-e-n-t-le, gentle.
- Pause every so often to talk about the story.

After reading

- Talk about what has been read.

Jen

Rav

Tess

1

The crew of the sub were lost. "There's something funny going on with my map," Rav said.

"It's getting a bit chilly," Jen said.
Tess tapped the window. "Look. Ice!"

"Time to get our sweaters on!" Rav said.

"Look out! Iceberg ahead!" Tess yelled.
The sub swerved, just missing the giant block.

Shards of ice hit the sub.
"We need to get out of danger!" Jen told them.

2

At the top, they looked out in amazement.
The sun glinted off the curved metal sub,
but the air was cold.

They were encircled by a blanket
of white ice and snow.

"There's no phone signal," Jen said.
"No one lives on this ice block," Rav replied.

"Who made those tread marks then?" Tess
wondered. "Maybe they can help us."

They got out and headed off, following the trail in the snow.

The tracks led to some huge metal domes.

A man called Larry was working there.
"I can fix your sub map," he said.
"I need help too! There are noises under
the ice. I think a whale is trapped."

The crew raced to the sub with Larry.
They dived through shards of ice.

"I can see something in that cave ahead," Rav said.

A spiky metal fence was blocking the cave's entrance. A young whale was trapped!

"You were right about the noise," Tess told Larry.
"We can solve this!" Jen said.

Tess and Rav swam through the icy water.
They fixed hooks to the metal fence.

Jen powered up the sub. With a gentle pull on the cable, the fence shifted.

The young whale raced out of the cave.

The whale circled the sub and swam off.
"Job done!" Jen said. "We'll take the rubbish."

Larry helped them fix the sub map.
It was time to go home.